Children Believe Everythi

Jennifer Day has worked with children and teenagers throughout the world for over twenty-five years within the performing and creative arts and in the fields of stress management and human potential. Her first book *Creative Visualization with Children – A Practical Guide* (Element, 1994) is being utilized by parents, teachers and counsellors around the world. She is the proud mother of Tammy (18), and lives in Hawaii where she directs Family Empowerment Retreats and offers workshops and seminars for parents and educators.

by the same author
Creative Visualization with Children

Children
Believe
Everything
You Say

CREATING
SELF-ESTEEM
WITH
CHILDREN

Jennifer Day

Illustrations byTammy Day-Ferraz

ELEMENT
Shaftesbury, Dorset • Rockport, Massachusetts
Brisbane, Queensland

First published in Great Britain in 1997 by
Element Books Limited
Shaftesbury, Dorset SP7 8BP

Published in the USA in 1997 by
Element Books, Inc.
PO Box 830, Rockport, MA 01966

Published in Australia in 1997 by
Element Books Limited
for Jacaranda Wiley Limited
33 Park Road, Milton, Brisbane 4064

Cover design by Mark Slader
Typeset by Bournemouth Colour Press, Parkstone, Poole, Dorset
Printed and bound in USA by Edwards Brothers Inc Michigan

British Library Cataloguing in Publication
data available

Library of Congress Cataloging in Publication
data available

ISBN 1–85230–958–X

Contents

Acknowledgements   ix

Introduction   1
Creating Self-Esteem with Children   1
Since Time Began   7

PART I PARENTING TODAY

1   **Children Believe Everything You Say**   11
2   **Personal Coping Tools for Parents**   14

**PART II SEVEN STEPS TO SELF-ESTEEM
       WITH CHILDREN**

Using Stories, Games, Imagery and Other Tools

3   **Step One: Developing Self-Awareness**   23
A Classic Tale: *I Will Stay at Home*   24
A Tale from India: *The Precious Stone*   26
A Game: *I Am Lovable and Capable*   28
A Game: *When I See, I Feel*   29

A Tool: *Being in the Heart*   30
A Tool: *Journal of the Heart*   31
A Tool: *Head and Heart Journal*   32
An Activity: *I Am Special*   33
A Visualization: *The Garden*   33

4 **Step Two: Managing Perception and Stress**   36
A Story from Arabia: *A Point of View*   37
A Native American Story: *Jumping Mouse*   39
A Game: *How Clear is your Reception?*   42
A Tool: *Heart Answers*   43
A Tool: *'What Then?' Map*   45
A Visualization: *Clouds of Perception*   46

5 **Step Three: Wishes, Dreams, Goals and
   Achievements**   48
A Story from Hawaii: *Holua-Manu*   49
A Story: *The Wishing Tree*   56
A Game: *Time Lines*   58
A Tool: *Treasure Album*   60
A Tool: *A 'Personal Plan' Tree*   61
A Visualization: *Your Theatre*   61

6 **Step Four: Fulfilment and Appreciation**   65
A Story from China: *The Stonecutter*   66
A Story from England: *The Young Oak Tree*   69
A Game: *Collage*   73
A Tool: *100 Blessings*   73
A Tool: *Gift*   74
A Visualization: *Heart Mail*   74

7   Step Five: Family and Relationship Dynamics   76
    A Story: *The Large and Beautiful Palace*   77
    Your Story: *Attention Parents!*   80
    A Game: *The Talking Stick*   80
    A Visualization: *Heart to Heart*   82
    A Tool: *Heart-to-Heart Listening*   83

8   Step Six: Community – Self-Care and
    Other-Care   85
    A Story: *The Prophecy*   86
    A Story: *Chopsticks*   87
    A Game: *Three's a Team*   89
    A Game: *If I Were a Colour*   89
    A Visualization: *Future Image*   90

9   Step Seven: The Earth – Global Awareness   93
    A Story from Indonesia: *Heart of Gold*   93
    A Story from India: *The Banyan Tree*   95
    A Game: *Webbing*   98
    A Game: *Leaves*   99
    A Visualization and Activity: *The Earth*   100
    A Visualization: *Planet Heart*   102

Finding More Tools   104

Recommended Further Reading   106

Useful Addresses   108

Index   118

This book is dedicated to all children, everywhere

Acknowledgements

First, I would like to thank my daughter Tammy for her beautiful illustrations for this book (and for my last book *Creative Visualization with Children*). Tammy demonstrates her imagination and her heart in such glorious ways and is a continuous source of inspiration to me and to all who know her! I would also like to thank all the families I have had the privilege to work with, know and love, especially Amber Grimm and the Grimm family. I want to thank my partner Grahame Clarke for giving me all the support I needed to write this book and for his unconditional love; my 'sister' Kay Snow-Davis for her immeasurable generosity of spirit; Serge Kahili King for his faith (and the computer!); Katrama Brooks for *Heart Talk* and for allowing me space for exploration; Jeff Goelitz for his heartfelt and enthusiastic support; Doc Lew Childre for his inspiration and for writing the best parenting book on the market; and Dr Deborah Rozman and everyone at the Institute of HeartMath for clarifying the heart perspective and inspiring the heart focus in this book, and for all their support. To my publisher,

Michael Mann, a very special thank you, and last but not least my deepest thanks to all the authors and teachers who have contributed to this book with their invaluable work.

A special thank you to all the authors and publishers who have given permission to quote from and reproduce stories and other copyright material. They include the following.

Values and Visions by Georgeanne Lamont and Sally Burns, Manchester Development Education Project, for 'I Am Lovable and Capable', 'When I See I Feel', 'Time Lines', 'Leaves', 'The Banyan Tree', 'The Prophecy', 'Chopsticks', and excerpts from *Positive Indian Parenting*. *Sharing Nature with Children* by J. Cornell, Exley Publications Ltd, for 'Webbing'. *Inside Stories* by Robin Richardson and Angela Wood, Trentham Books, for 'Five Journeys', 'The Stonecutter', 'I'm Staying Here', 'The Precious Stone', and for a version of 'A Point of View'. *Kauai Tales* by Frederick B. Wichman, Bamboo Ridge Press, for 'Holua-Manu'. *Notes to My Children* by Ken Carey, Uni Sun, for 'Jumping Mouse' and a version of 'The Wishing Tree'. *Teaching Children Joy* by Linda and Richard Eyre, Ballantine Books, for 'I Am Special' and a version of 'The Young Oak Tree'. *The Ultimate Kid* by Jeffrey Goelitz, Planetary Publications, for 'What Then?' and a version of 'How Clear is Your Reception'. *For The Fun Of It!* by Marta Harrison and The Nonviolence and Children Program, Friends Peace Committee, for 'If I Were a Colour' and a version of 'Three's a Team'.

Jennifer Day

Introduction

Creating self-esteem with children

Much has been written on the subject of self-esteem during recent years, some of it controversial and much of it valuable and in many cases transformational. Fortunately, most parents today recognize that children (and indeed all human beings) need a solid base of self-confidence and esteem to be able to function as healthy, balanced, successful individuals in today's complex society. However, recognizing this can be frustrating unless we have tools to actively help our children build such a base. Overwhelmed as we often are by juggling domestic difficulties, professional problems and financial uncertainties within seemingly unreasonable time limits, child-rearing can appear daunting. The challenges facing parents today are probably greater than at any other time in history. Never before have we had to raise children surrounded by the profound changes and the constant state of flux existing within our society and throughout the world.

1

There is no course of study that prepares parents, or children, for the increasing levels of stress we are experiencing. There is no curriculum that gives parents the tools or the support to raise happy, well-adjusted children in today's society – children who have the self-esteem necessary to make healthy effective choices in an increasingly volatile world.

Yet tools do exist, support can be obtained, and we *can* help our children to build the self-esteem they so sorely need – and we can do it within the limitations of our own hectic lives.

One of the most powerful, simple, fast and readily available tools is the imagination. Guiding the imagination *consciously*, through the language we use, through story and through imagery, we can create our own integrated 'parenting curriculum', not only for building self-esteem, but for teaching, implementing and sustaining family values – also sorely needed in today's world. Another equally if not more powerful tool is the heart. Through a *conscious* focus on the heart and feelings of love, care, compassion, humour and appreciation we create the strongest antidote to stress – the greatest adversary of self-esteem and family values. The two tools integrate together. Imagery is frequently the most effective way to access the heart, and the heart is the most effective way to alter negative or detrimental images and perceptions.

We think in images all the time. As you are reading this, images are flashing across your mind at the speed of – or faster than – a movie. If you don't 'see' the images, you either 'hear' them or you 'sense' them. In some way, we all 'visualize' constantly, from the day we are born until the day we die. How we utilize this inborn ability determines how we perceive the events of our lives and in turn how we react to and experience life.

Most adult imaginations today are controlled by What ifs: 'What if I get ill?', 'What if I can't pay the bills?', 'What if someone saw me run the red light?' And when our children are very young, we teach them to do the same. We conjure up images, in detail, to keep our children from getting hurt or to enforce discipline: 'Be careful or you'll fall and hurt yourself!'; 'If you're not careful, a car will run you over and you'll have to go to hospital'; 'If you don't study hard, you'll fail and then what will become of you? You'll ____!' (please feel free to fill in the blank space). Unfortunately, we do not spend nearly as much time or attention on giving our children *positive* images.

Our children grow up hearing their parents say things like, 'I'm sick to death of it!', 'He's a pain in the neck!', 'She's at boiling point!', 'It's just not good enough!', 'You'll be the death of me!' and 'I need this like a hole in the head!' Imagine for a moment the images that go through a toddler's mind on hearing remarks like these.

The imagination is a powerful element of our being. If you were in a room with a plank lying across the floor and you were asked to walk across the plank, the chances are that you would be able to execute this with little trouble. However, if the plank were to be suspended between two poles twenty feet above the ground you would probably find it somewhat more challenging. This is because your imagination would begin to play 'What if?' tapes in your mind. When these 'tapes' are strong enough, they will affect your confidence, your balance and your ability to perform the task.

The imagination also has a *direct* effect on your body. Imagine for a moment a lemon. Imagine holding it and feeling the waxy, uneven texture of the peel. Smell the bitter-sweet, distinct smell of the peel. Imagine placing the lemon on a table in front of you and slicing the lemon in half. Now lift one half of the lemon slowly up to your lips, open your mouth and bite into the lemon. Feel how the juices explode in your mouth. More likely than not, you are now salivating. Although it is not always as obvious, every one of your mind's images has an effect on your physical body.

One of the first things I noticed when I began working with children was how easily stress manifests itself in their young bodies. Already in first grade, if peers or teachers cause stress for a child it shows up first in the child's body: tense shoulders, stooped posture, bowed head, etc. The tension in a child's body will increase in direct proportion to the fearful or anxiety producing images in his or her mind. Stress amongst children is reaching epidemic proportions in our society, as it is amongst adults. In terms of building self-esteem, stress rates as the number one deterrent.

Stress, in children and adults, is the results of how we *perceive* a situation in our minds. Stress is not – as a common belief – a result of the situation itself. Stress is the result of our *perception* of the situation and is the body's reaction to fears, assumptions and, more often than not, projections about our future – 'what ifs?' that we conjure up in our minds. The more vivid these images are, the greater the stress will be. The greater the stress, the more insecure we become about our ability to handle it and the less we believe in our own personal coping abilities. The result is lower self-image; the lower our self-image and self-esteem sinks, the more likely we are to perceive a situation as stressful. It becomes a never-ending cycle.

We can, however, learn to harness our imagination and use our inborn ability for creating images to *prevent* stress rather than to cause it. We can increase our level of awareness and become conscious of how we use imagery in daily life. We can develop visualization as a skill to improve the quality of our lives and the lives of our children. We can use imagery as a tool to *communicate* with our children, to build a positive self-image, and to help us be more effective parents.

The conscious use of imagery to teach and raise children is not new; most cultures have recognized the power of the imagination and have used legends, stories and visualization to teach children throughout the ages (see 'Since Time Began', p. 7).

This book provides a collection of tales, stories, awareness games and processes, suggested resources and creative visualizations to support key areas of parenting, teaching children coping skills and values, building self-esteem, and strengthening the family. It offers a variety of different ways to focus and develop the imagination and the heart as positive tools for the improvement and enhancement of life; your children's and your own. Everything in this book has been tried and tested countless times, in families (my own included!), groups, workshops and counselling situations – always with great results.

Part I consists of personal coping tools for parents designed to support the skills you have already have; to improve your ability for self-care (making you better able to care for others); and to help you see life from your child's point of view, thereby making it simpler for you to effectively guide him or her. Part 2 consists of stories, games and guided imagery for your children, your family – and yourself.

Each chapter in Part II carries a specific theme, although all the chapters have the underlying common denominator of love. Each chapter leaves room for expansion, creativity and play. All the stories, games and processes are designed to be easily integrated into family life, however busy you may be. You might like to begin by choosing your favourite story, game or process, and planning the easiest time to introduce it; this could be at the dinner table, at bedtime, on a Sunday morning, or instead of your least favourite TV show. As you discover the most comfortable way and time for *you and your family* to use these tools, you will naturally and gradually expand their use until they become an integrated part of your lives. Eventually you will find yourself picking up other stories and games to add to your collection.

The contents of this book are intended to initiate rather than lead, to facilitate rather than teach, to guide rather than inform and to inspire rather than tell. Most of all they are intended to make the process of creating self-esteem an enjoyable one.

Have fun!

Since Time Began

(from *Positive Indian Parenting*)

'Our people have been using legends as a way of teaching ever since time began. Legends were told only during the winter time, because that was the time for teaching, the time the children were inside the longest.

The story-teller was a man or woman who was well respected in the tribe. Sometimes they were parents or grandparents. The story-teller had to know the legends, history, be involved in tribal politics, religious ceremonies and be an excellent child psychologist. The story-teller had to learn to work well with groups and be able to sense the need of the audience. They could read children by just observing them.

There were many lessons in story-telling. Trickster stories, for example, have moral teachings. Raven stories are called 'Trickster Legends'. Story-telling brings generations together. The elders, parents and children all participated in the story-telling process. There were no generation gaps in our culture mostly because social functions were not age exclusive. Story-telling is an example.

Most legends stress that one should not be greedy, boastful, or make fun of others, especially elders, and that small beings could outsmart bigger and stronger beings. The legends also encourage older children to watch out for and help younger and weaker children. In this way legends taught the right way to do things.'

PART I

Parenting
Today

Chapter 1

Children Believe Everything You Say

Small children listen, absorb and believe everything their parents say. As they grow older they might not listen as well or believe *everything* you say, but they will still absorb it. If there is much shouting or verbal abuse in the home it will teach the children that this is an appropriate form of communication. (Studies have shown that children from verbally abusive homes are much more likely to become verbally abusive themselves than children from non-abusive homes.) Children will also absorb – and sometimes even take literally – abusive language that is not necessarily *meant* to be abusive. For example, 'He's such a pain!' or 'She'll be the death of me!' Recent studies have also shown that such language can actually contribute to physical ailments.

When I became aware of this, a number of years ago, I had been suffering from acute neck pains on a regular basis. Various treatments helped but nothing *cured* it. I began to keep a journal every time I suffered these neck pains. Soon a pattern became apparent and I discovered that my neck pains were always most acute after meetings with a certain colleague of mine. I examined my thoughts about him and realized (to my amusement) that I had been thinking of this man as being a 'pain in the neck'. Once aware of the imagery I had been carrying around, I was able to change it. Eventually the neck pains disappeared!

Much of the imagery we project into our children is fear-based. However it doesn't have to be. We can change the way we express ourselves. It may take a little time and some practice, but seeing the difference it can make to our children makes it well worth the effort!

You can change the way you say something, using *positive* imagery to replace negative or fear-based imagery. Read through the following list of negative remarks and the suggested positive alternatives. Make your own list of negative remarks and see if you can find a positive way to rephrase each one.

Be careful or you'll fall down and hurt yourself.
Hold tight and you'll be safe.

If you don't study hard you'll fail.
If you study you'll pass all your tests.

You are driving me crazy.
I am becoming agitated by your behaviour.

Team up with a friend or your partner and keep a notebook or diary of each other's language for one week. Jot down all the negative and fear-based language you hear your partner using. At the end of the week, get together and compare notes. Discuss how you can best help each other to adjust to more positive phrasing. Such support is vital to effective change. Once your own awareness increases, involve your children too. Ask them for suggestions on how to improve phrasing, and look for ways to create family language awareness. Make it a team effort. Avoid 'lecturing' or 'telling' your children – after all, most of their negative language was probably picked up from you or another adult! The best teacher is always *example*.

Once your awareness of language is heightened, you will discover an increase in your awareness of the images your carry in your mind and the images you project onto others and the future. As you develop this new awareness, a new world opens up to you, a world in which you can take charge of your life and help your children take charge of theirs.

Chapter 2

Personal Coping Tools for Parents

Your Personal Imagery

Take ten minutes each day – just before you go to bed can be a good time – to focus your own imagination on the qualities that you *appreciate* about your children. Remember an enjoyable episode or a special event that you enjoyed as a family. Focus on that for a few minutes. Try not to let your mind get in the way with other thoughts. If this happens, just let the thoughts drift by like clouds in the sky and bring your focus back to the enjoyable memory. Stay focused on your chosen imagery or memory as if it were a photograph. *Enjoy* the feeling. See if you can make it spread throughout your entire body until you feel like one big smile!

Handling Your Own Anger

Whenever you feel yourself becoming angry with your child, take twenty seconds of 'time-out' and push the pause button on your anger. Think of something you appreciate about your child. Focus only on the feeling of appreciation for twenty seconds or so. When you come back to reclaim your anger you may find it looks different. You will probably also find that your response will be more objective and less emotional. This may take a little practice, but don't give up! It's well worth the effort. One small tip: the longer you let your anger build up before you 'push pause', the more difficult it will be. *As soon as* you feel yourself becoming angry – 'push pause'. If this feels difficult or impossible to do, see 'Managing Stress', p. 17.

Giving Unspoken Support

Whenever your child is having difficulty with something, and you are not in a position to help out, take a moment to be still and focus on your own heart. Take some of the love you have for him in your heart and send it to him. Imagine it beaming out from your heart to his and back to you. Imagine how good it makes him feel and enjoy how good it makes you feel.

You do not have to be within close physical proximity to do this. Nor do you have to wait until your child is having a problem. You can do this on a regular basis. See if you can monitor the effect it has on him and whether it makes a difference to your relationship.

Your Image of Your Child

What is the image you hold of your child? Are there judgements involved, or assessments? Do you *expect* bad or unruly behaviour at times? Take a moment – while you're driving, cleaning or gardening are good moments – to hold an image of your child in the near future. If could be later that same day, the next day or a week later. Imagine her response to something specific, a challenge maybe. Imagine it as positive and as perfect for her as you can. See her responding with ease, grace and a resulting satisfaction, contentment or happiness. Make your image as vivid as you can. Include colours, sounds, tastes and smells. Focus on the perfect scenario and *expect* it to happen.

If your mind projects a more negative scenario, replace it with the perfect, positive one. Put your heart into it, using feelings of appreciation for your child to fuel it.

Should your child *not* react as you visualized, do not let yourself become disappointed. Focus instead on whatever positive qualities you can find in the situation. Let your child know how much you love her, no matter what.

Your Perception

If you feel you do not understand your child or you are in conflict with him, take a moment to 'switch places' in your imagination. Place yourself in your child's shoes for a few seconds. How does the situation look to him?

This insight may help you to resolve the situation by gaining an understanding of *both* perceptions – yours and your child's.

Managing Stress

Firstly, always remember that in order for you to help your children manage their stress, you have to be able to manage your own. Now ask yourself two questions: where in your body do you take your stress? And what do you do to release and relieve your stress?

Although the ideal situation would be to avoid a stress reaction altogether, the reality is that we aren't always able to do that. Stress occurs – and then what? There are three Rs to managing stress that are easy to remember: Release, Relieve and Relax.

Once you have had a stress reaction, it is vital that the tension and stress be *released* physically. Our bodies are designed to perform a physical activity in response to stress. If we don't, the adrenaline released into our blood stream during a stress reaction becomes toxic to the body. Therefore, having experienced stress, the best release is exercise; for example, go for a run, punch a punching bag or do jumping jacks. If the whole family has experienced a stress reaction, and a feeling of anger or resentment is in the air, I have found that a short 'family tantrum' is both an appropriate and healthy release. Jump up and down together, shout and scream if you want, and lie down and pound the floor with your fists. This usually ends in fits of laughter and has the dual effect of dissolving the negative mood and releasing everybody's stress!

The second R, *relieve*, is easy to execute once you know where in your body you take your stress. If you have a hard time identifying this, ask your partner or a friend to help. Once identified, make sure you find a way to relieve the tension after a stress reaction. When you have *released* the stress, *relieve* your tense body with a brief massage (i.e. a shoulder rub), a hot bath or a yoga class. As a family you can give each other shoulder rubs, do yoga together or just play some soft music on the stereo.

To *relax* and *revitalize* yourself after a stress reaction is not always easy. I have found the best and most effective way to do this is to relax gently into the heart. Focus all your awareness on your heart and think of something or someone that you really appreciate. Focus on that image for a minute and feel yourself relaxing and being re-energized. As a family, you can guide each other through this process (I elaborate more on this in later chapters) with some calm music in the background, and maybe the promise of a nice cup of tea!

The three Rs to managing stress need not take more than a few minutes altogether. If you choose to use this as a family tool, write *Release, Relieve and Relax* on a brightly coloured piece of paper and put it on your refrigerator door to help you remember.

When you are able to identify warning signs *before* a stress reaction, the best way to *avoid* it altogether is to go straight to *'Relax' gently into the heart.* It will change your physical, mental and emotional reactions and support you in preventing stress and managing the situation in question from a more objective viewpoint.

The following are some de-stressing hints to help you manage your stress. Choose five of them that you feel you can really commit to, write them down on a piece of paper, and stick them where you are likely to see them often. Then *use them!*

Take time to smile
Take time to appreciate one thing in your life
Do a relaxation exercise – daily!
Have a massage
Talk to a friend
Read a story to your child
Stroke an animal
Take time out and 'go to your heart'
Switch activities
Be nice to yourself
Identify stress behaviour
Accept your limits
Plan a fun day
Share a success with your child
Identify stress thinking
Let your imagination free-float
Exercise daily
De-stress between work and home
Spend time in your heart
Limit time spent on a crisis
Give your child a hug
Do a creative visualization
Say 'no' to a demand

Say 'yes' to a break
Congratulate yourself
Admire a view
Enjoy nature
Do something creative with your child
Remember the three Rs of managing stress
Give CHANGE a chance!

PART II

Seven Steps to Self-Esteem with Children

Using Stories,
Games, Imagery
and Other Tools

Chapter 3

Step One:
Developing
Self-Awareness

Learning to understand our own emotions is the first step to finding inner peace and stillness, and to learning to love and care for ourselves. These abilities are essential if we are to manage stress, build self-esteem, follow our dreams, develop meaningful relationships and become effective, contributing and caring members of our communities – in short, if we are to function with a measurable degree of happiness in today's society.

Unfortunately, much of society teaches us to look *outside* of ourselves for our gratification and happiness. As we try to satisfy ourselves with 'things' and 'quick fixes' from outside ourselves, we only want more. This method can never completely satisfy or fulfil us, for we are placing our confidence in everything but our 'self'. What we are *really seeking* is the unshakeable confidence (*self*-confidence) that comes only with self-knowledge and care and knowing we can handle what life has to offer.

The earlier a child begins to develop this awareness of self and an understanding of his emotions, the less likely he will be to look 'outside' for gratification, and the less emotional 'luggage' he will have to off-load as an adult. The younger a child is when he learns to care for and love himself, the stronger this self-love – and love for others – will be in adult years. Very young children are often reflective and have a sense of stillness and contemplation. As soon as a child has reconnected with the joy and pleasure of inner peace and reflection, he will have a coping tool for life that is immeasurable in value.

A Classic Tale:

I Will Stay at Home

Once upon a time there were three sisters. As soon as they were grown up each one decided to search for truth and purpose in her own way. The first sister said, 'I'm going to take care of the sick and the poor. The streets in the cities are full of them. I will bring them healing and I will care for them.'

The second sister said, 'Everywhere I look I see people in conflict, people fighting with each other, people at war. I will go to them and reconcile them. I will talk to them and bring them peace.'

The third sister said, 'I will stay at home.'

A few years passed and the first two sisters returned home. The first sister sighed and said, 'It's hopeless! There are simply too many sick, poor and homeless people. I cannot cope!'

The second sister moaned and said, 'It's impossible to make peace between people. I am completely worn out.' They both slumped down in their chairs and sat exhausted, looking at each other in despair.

At first the third sister said nothing. Then she quietly filled a bowl with muddy water. 'Look into that,' she said. 'Just look.'

The two sisters looked but they saw nothing, only muddy water. 'Let it stand,' their sister said. 'Let it be.'

After a while they looked again. The water was clear now, and they saw their own reflections in it as clearly as in a mirror. The third sister told them, 'When the water is stirred up it is muddy and you can see nothing. But when the water is very still it becomes clear. It is the same with human beings. You can see clearly only when you are still, very still. Only when you are still and can see yourself can you also see what you should do, and where you should go.

'Look into the water.'

Only in stillness can you have hope and faith in the future, and in your own talents, abilities and creativity. Only then can you throw yourself wholeheartedly and with love into caring for others. Only then can you be unconcerned about rewards or the fruits or your actions. Only then can you truly act from your heart.'

A Tale from India:

The Precious Stone

It was dusk and the air was still, as the wandering holy man settled under a tree, near the big rock, beside the path, at the foot of the mountain. There he would spend the night, with a stone for a pillow. He had few belongings and had long ago given up the idea of becoming successful, or making a lot of money, or even becoming very popular. He had whatever he needed and he needed very little. He had left the world in order to find himself without it. His evening meditation was disturbed by the shouts of a businessman who came running up to him in an agitated state, 'It must be you, I'm sure it must be you!' he blurted out. 'I had a dream last night telling me to come to this tree, near the big rock, beside the path, at the foot of the mountain. Here a wandering holy man would give me a priceless stone and I would be rich forever!'

'I've been looking for you all day,' he added.

The precious stone

'Searching, searching, searching. I'm so glad now that I've found you!'

'Perhaps this jewel is the stone from your dream,' said the holy man, rummaging in his bag and pulling out a sparkling rock. 'I happened to see it on the path. Do take it.'

The businessman's mouth dropped open in amazement and his eyes grew large with delight. He had never seen such a huge diamond, and never even dreamed that a diamond could be so enormous. As he carried it away to his home he glowed with satisfaction and fulfilment. His long day of searching had not been in vain. But the felling did not last very long and by the end of the evening he was deeply troubled. He tossed and turned all night and couldn't get to sleep. He wanted to plan what he would do with his new riches, and how he would enjoy all his new possessions and wealth, and all the new opportunities life now had in store for him. But he

27

couldn't get the wandering holy man out of his mind, what had happened that day and what it might all mean.

Before dawn broke he got up and went back to the tree, near the big rock, beside the path, at the foot of the mountain. Disturbing the holy man's morning meditation, he laid the diamond before him. And he asked, 'Please, can I have the precious gift that made you give away this stone?'

A Game:

I Am Lovable and Capable

You will need: a pair of scissors, blue tack, and for each family member two sheets of paper and some colour pencils.

As a family, talk about the fact that we are all born believing we are lovable and capable. However, as we grow and interact with others, we are often given cause to believe otherwise. This activity can help us to identify our emotional responses and reaffirm that we really are lovable and capable.

Give each family member a sheet of paper and have them draw a self-portrait. Colour it and make it as detailed as you want. Then have each person take the second sheet of paper and write, in capital letters, I AM LOVABLE AND CAPABLE several times and then cut out each word and stick the words onto or around their self-portrait. Have each person hang their portraits up near their bed. Set a time period (i.e. one week) and during that time, whenever a person feels hurt or sad or angry or bad, he or she takes one (or more, depending on the strength of feeling) word off their portrait. Likewise, each time a person feels good, he or she puts a word back onto the portrait.

At the end of the pre-set time period, have everyone come together and share their experiences. Try not to make judgements or have discussions, just share and honour everyone's *feelings!* You can use this as an on-going activity, indefinitely.

<u>A Game:</u>

When I See, I Feel

This can be done anywhere, even while driving, with two or more people.

One person says 'When I see ____' (for example 'a kitten'). The second person continues 'I feel ____' (expressing what a kitten makes her feel). Then the second person says 'When I see ____' (for example 'garbage on the street'). The third (or first, if there are only two) person continues 'I feel ____' (whatever garbage on the street makes him feel), and so on.

You can also use 'When I hear ____'. Do not be afraid to utilize an array of images to connect with as many feelings as possible. Permit yourself to set an example using vivid and clear images and expressions.

Never discount a child's feelings. The feelings of a child may sometimes seem trivial or silly to an adult, but these feelings are very real to the child. If a child expresses sadness or anger, encourage her to acknowledge these feelings and help her to understand them. 'When I see, I feel' can be especially useful with children who suppress or discount their own emotions.

<u>A Tool:</u>

Being in the Heart

Whenever you're feeling a little sad or lonely, it helps to go into your heart to make yourself feel better. However, this isn't always easy. For most people it is a concept that is hard to practise in real life.

Here is one way you can help your child(ren), and yourself, to connect with the heart. You can also use it with children to help them go to sleep. If for some reason it doesn't work straight away, keep practising. The heart is like a muscle – it needs 'building'.

When you use the following script, or otherwise guide your child in a visualization, speak slowly, softly and audibly. Remember to pause between sentences so that all you say can be completely absorbed.

'Close your eyes for a moment and take a few

really deep breaths, all the way down into your stomach. Try to let go of any tension in your body. If you have something on your mind, press the "pause" button, like on your video machine. You can get back to it in a moment. Now focus all your attention on the area around your heart. Keep focusing on that area and see if you can feel your heart beating.

Now think of something you love, or a memory that makes you feel good. Maybe it's a favourite place, a pet, an event, a game or a special hug. It can be anything you want, anything that makes you feel love. Now keep thinking that thought and feel what happens to your heart. How does it feel? Keep holding the thought and the feeling in your heart. Enjoy it for just a moment, and then see if you can spread that feeling all around your body, filling yourself up with energy from your heart.

Now, whenever your's ready, you can open your eyes.'

A Tool:

Journal of the Heart

After doing the 'being in the Heart' process, have each child (and adults too!) keep a journal. Write down the first thoughts that come to you as you open your eyes, and then your journal. Be sure to remember that everyone's journal is *private!*

A Tool:

Head and Heart Journal

You and your child(ren) might also like to keep part of your journal as a 'Head and Heart Journal'. At the top of every left-hand page write 'Head Page', at the top of every right-hand page write 'Heart Page'. Whenever something is bothering your child, when she's upset about something or she is feeling angry, have her take out the journal and write down all her feelings and thoughts on the left-hand 'Head' page(s). Remember, this is a *private* journal. Let your child write anything she wants, *all* her thoughts, no matter how unacceptable she thinks they are, *you are not going to read them.* When she has finished, have her put down her journal for a moment and either close her eyes or focus on something pretty like a flower. Ask her to think for a moment about something she loves; it can be anything – as in the 'Being in the Heart' process – a puppy, a cup of cocoa, a soccer game, a hug, the ocean, or whatever makes her feel good. Then ask her to notice the feeling she gets. How does it make her heart feel? Ask her to hold onto and enjoy that feeling for a moment. Then ask her to open her eyes, pick up her journal and write her thoughts – from the heart – on the right-hand 'Heart' page. Ask her to just write the first thing that comes to her. When she has finished, ask her to compare the two pages and see if her thoughts about the situation that upset her haven't changed a little.

I Am Special

You will need: six to eight sheets of paper per person, pencils, colour crayons, a stapler, scissors, glue, personal photos and memorabilia.

Have each family member put their sheets of paper together, fold them once and staple them together on the fold, to make a book. Title the book 'I Am Special' or 'I Love Me'.

Have each person fill their book with as much information and memorabilia about themselves as possible. Each person can start their book with basic information such as name, date of birth, astrological sign, hair colour, height, etc. Continue with lists like 'Why I Like Me', '20 Things I Love About Me', '10 Things I Like To Do', 'Things That Make Me Special', etc. Have everyone draw, colour, and stick photos, lockets of hair and memorabilia in their books, filling them with as much *special* and *loving* information about themselves as they can.

The Garden

Have your child(ren) breathe deeply and evenly and focus on a point in front of them and slightly upwards. As they focus on this point, suggest that they may be feeling their eyelids becoming heavier. Tell them to close their eyes as soon as it feels natural. Read the following script to them, making sure your voice is calm, soft and audible. Try not to sound monotonous, and pause regularly so that all you say may be absorbed.

Gently place your hand on your heart and listen for your heartbeat. Feel the rhythm – is it slowing down or is it even?... Keep all your attention on your heart. If other thoughts enter your mind, just let them float on by like petals on a river and bring your attention right back to your heart. Now, holding your attention there, think of someone or something that you love – maybe a hug or a puppy – feel what that thought does to your heart. How does that make you feel? Hold that feeling in your heart for a little while, really hold onto it. Enjoy how nice it feels.

Now I want you to see before you a path in nature... it can be any way you want it to be – wide, narrow, winding, straight, by a stream or by the sea, in a forest or in the mountains – whatever you like. Now I want you to walk down your path until you come to a tree, a tree with many branches. This is your Trouble Tree, the tree where you hang all your troubles. Pause for a moment and offload all your troubles – no matter how small. Hang them all on the tree before you move on.... Now continue on down your path. If there are any rocks or twigs or other obstacles, stop and gently move them to the side. Give them some of all that love you have in your heart and move on. Soon you arrive at a small gate covered in your favourite flowers.

Smell their lovely fragrance as you gently push open the gate. As you step through your gate you enter into the most beautiful garden you have ever seen. It is exactly the way you want it to be and it is all your very own... all the colours in your garden are very bright and beautiful. The sun is shining, the birds are singing a welcoming song and you feel very safe and peaceful here. Wander through your garden for a while, exploring... [pause]

Now before you leave, I want you to thank your garden for being there for you and for being so perfect. Know that your garden will always be there for you whenever you need it... Now gradually bring your attention back to your heart ... Has your heartbeat changed at all? Feel the love inside your heart and send it all around your body. Feel how good that feels. Now bring your attention to your breathing. Has it slowed down? Very gradually bring your attention back into this room, and whenever you are ready, you can open your eyes.

Chapter 4

Step Two: Managing Perception and Stress

One of the most difficult things for most of us to accept is that *our perception determines our response to any given situation.* It is difficult to accept because this concept makes us totally responsible for our own reactions and therefore for our own reality. For example, we can feel stressed about our child's low grades at school, worry, loose sleep, make our blood pressure go up and let it affect our mood for hours. Or, we can let it go, realizing that to feel stressed about it will not help the situation or our child, and that we are probably better equipped to guide our child from a state of calm objectivity. The choice we make between these two approaches, or perceptions, will determine our response, the response of our child, and the reality that follows.

We have a *choice.* We can choose how we perceive the events of our lives; a cup is either half full or half empty depending on our perception. We can choose to take complete responsibility for our own actions and reactions and teach our children to do the same. We can help our children – both by guidance and by example – to understand *perception* before they become adults, hence empowering them to take charge of their own responses and avoid much of the stress, conflicts and victim consciousness so prevalent in our society today.

<u>A Story from Arabia:</u>

A Point of View

Once upon a time there was a large ship that set sail on a very rough sea. All the men on board were sailors and sons of sailors, and all of them had seen many rough seas – all except one, that is. Not only had he never seen rough seas before, he had never been on a boat of any kind, nor even ever learned to swim.

He began to feel queasy as soon as they left the harbour. As the ship rolled, so did his stomach, as the ship heaved so did he. By the time land was out of sight and a fierce storm had begun to blow up he was quite green. He hung over the side of the ship moaning loudly. 'I can't take any more,' he groaned. 'I want to get off!' Soon his groans became cries. 'Let me off, let me off!' he cried.

At first the other sailors ignored him. After a while a few of them asked him to pull himself together. Eventually one sailor tried to calm him down by

A ship set sail on a rough sea

telling him he would eventually get his sea legs and admitting that he too had once felt like that. But nothing helped and finally he became quite hysterical. The captain could stand it no more 'Will somebody please do something about him!' he bellowed.

'He says he wants to get off,' the second mate responded. 'I think we should oblige him.' And with that he grabbed the man's legs, the skipper grabbed his arms, and together they threw him overboard.

The sea was not only rough but cold as well. The man was terrified and convinced he was drowning. He began to panic, thrashing around wildly and screaming louder than ever.

It is said that when you come face to face with death, your whole life flashes before you. Well, that is what happened to the man. As he thrashed about, gasping for air, he remembered his nearest and dearest and the sweetest moments of his life.

He had not noticed that everyone on board ship had gathered at the side of the deck and were leaning over watching him. Nor did he notice the skipper signal to two of the sailors, who subsequently jumped into the water and pulled him out.

He didn't drown. When they got him on board they brought him a hot drink and wrapped him in blankets. He soon calmed down and was back to normal.

The captain turned to the second mate and said, 'I know I asked you to do something about him, but wasn't that a little extreme? Although,' he added, glancing at the now calm, contented young man, 'it seems to have worked.'

'Well you see, captain,' replied the second mate, 'it wasn't until he was drowning that he realized how safe the ship was. Everything depends on your point of view, I always think, don't you sir?'

A Native American Story:

Jumping Mouse

Once upon a time there was a field mouse by the name of Jumping Mouse. Jumping Mouse used to run and play with all the other mice, nibbling on this, nibbling on that, scurrying here, scurrying there, doing all the little things that mice do. Jumping Mouse thought it was all quite boring so every so often he would jump up in the air. That is how he got the name Jumping Mouse.

When Jumping Mouse jumped, he could see much further than the other mice because he was higher up. From up in the air he could see way past all the little mousy goings on that all the other mice were concerned with. From up high he could see hills and mountains and tree tops. Whenever he landed after having seen something he had never seen before, he would rush to tell the other mice about it. They listened but showed very little interest because they were too busy being concerned about their mousy goings on, hurrying, scurrying, nibbling and worrying.

Jumping Mouse jumped more and more often, and each time he would see more and more things. He would see past all the little things the other mice were worrying about. The other mice were always worrying about whether they would have enough to eat and whether they would find dry shelter when it rained. They lived in a field with plenty to eat and many holes in the ground and trees which gave shelter. But still they worried.

The mice also worried about the great eagle and whether it would swoop down on them and eat them. Whenever they saw the eagle flying above they would all scurry into their holes and hide.

Now Jumping Mouse had two eyes just like the rest of us, but one of his eyes helped him to look at the past and the other eye helped him to see into the future. One day something poked the eye that looked at the past, so he could no longer be concerned with all that had happened before. The very next day something else poked the eye that saw into the future,

Jumping mouse

so he could no longer be concerned with what was going to happen next. Now he could only be concerned with what was happening at the moment. He could not scurry about like the other mice – even if he wanted to – worrying about the future and whether there would be enough, or thinking about the past and whether bad things would repeat themselves. He could only think about what was happening *now*.

One day the eagle came swooping down and of course Jumping Mouse didn't see him until he was

41

right there – and snatching him up. Then as if by magic, Jumping Mouse became the eagle. All at once Jumping Mouse was soaring through the sky and he could see everything there was to see across the earth, all the way to the horizon and back. He could see forever.

A Game:

How Clear is your Reception?

You will need: one sheet of paper each, pencils, colour crayons and a large hard-backed book (encyclopaedia size) or screen.

Divide up into pairs. Sit opposite each other at a table, with the screen up between you. Take one sheet of paper each, place it in front of your and be sure neither of you can see your partner's paper.

One person draws a picture – not too complicated. When you have finished, keep your eyes on your picture while describing it carefully to your partner who will then attempt to reproduce your drawing on his or her own sheet of paper. No hand signals or questions are allowed – nor is peeking! When you have finished, compare pictures and see just how well you communicated. Discuss what worked and what didn't. Change places and play again.

A Tool:

Heart Answers

You will need: red material (preferably felt), thick paper or card, scissors, a pen, a needle and thread.

Fold the material so that it is double thickness. Draw a heart on it, as big or bigger than your hand. Cut it out and sew the two hearts together, leaving a gap at the top large enough to put your hand into.

On the paper or card, draw up to 50 hearts, 1 or 2 inches wide each. Have each family member take an equal share of the hearts, cut them out, and write one 'Heart Answer' on each heart. Let everyone choose their favourite Heart Answers from the list below, or make up your own.

Finally, place all the Heart Answers in the material heart and mix them up. Whenever any one of you has a hard time getting in touch with your heart intuition (or inner knowing), or changing your perception to see something from a different point of view, hold the heart to your chest, close your eyes and be still for a moment, while you think of something that makes you go to your heart/feel love. Then 'ask the heart' a question regarding your perception or need for intuitive guidance. You can ask your question out loud or silently. Imagine your question going into the heart. Open your eyes, dip your hand into the heart, and pull out your Heart Answer!

Suggested Heart Answers

Enjoy today!
Practise compassion
What can *you* do to
  make it better?
Shine like the sun
Expect your wishes to
  come true
Use your imagination
You know!
Share what you know
Do things the heart way
Hold the thought and it
  will be real
Look in the mirror
Enjoy yourself
You have everything!
Feel the love around you
See it another way
Change your perception
Are you giving?
Follow your heart
Send love to where you
  hurt
You are loved
Let yourself laugh
You are perfect
You are good enough
Don't hang on, let go!
Be kind to someone
Help others

Let your fears fly away!
You are a child of love
Appreciate yourself
Be nice to yourself
Everything is in motion
Everything wants to be
  loved
Be flexible like a young
  tree
Don't worry, be happy!
Just do it!
Practise appreciation
Make your dreams come
  true
You make your reality
Stay in your heart
Think thoughts that
  make you feel good
Love yourself
Be fearless
Life is fun
Trust yourself
Practise forgiveness
Thank someone you love
Relax and try again
Feel how you are
  connected to everyone
Problems are there to be
  conquered
Don't stress. Have fun!

A Tool:

'What Then?' Map

Most people – both adults and children – worry. We especially worry about things that *might* happen.

Making a 'What Then?' Map can help you let go of the worrying, and the tension and stress that goes with it. You can make a 'What Then?' Map about any worry you might have. Here is a short example:

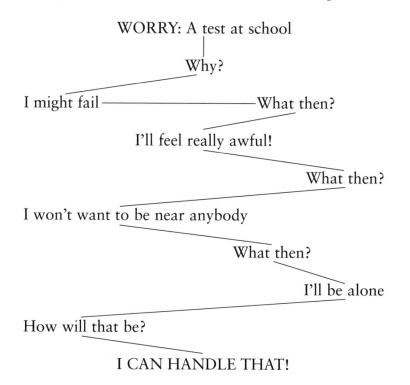

WORRY: A test at school

Why?

I might fail ——————— What then?

I'll feel really awful!

What then?

I won't want to be near anybody

What then?

I'll be alone

How will that be?

I CAN HANDLE THAT!

A 'What Then?' map

A Visualization:

Clouds of Perception

Guide your child as described in 'The Garden' visualization in Chapter 3, p. 33.

Breathe deeply into your stomach... and close your eyes. Now think of someone or something that makes your heart feel warm and full of love. As you hold this feeling, try to relax and clear your mind... Now imagine you are lying on a cool, dry grass lawn. You are looking up at the sky above you and you see a few small fluffy white clouds floating by. You watch them and discover that their shapes create many different images. In one cloud you see the figure of a lady, young and lovely. As you watch, the images change to that of an old witch, and then to an elf. You stay and watch the clouds for a little while and see how many different shapes and images they make as you look at them in different ways.

You can look at all kinds of things as if they were clouds. Try looking at someone you don't like in this way and see if you can see something different and good. [You can adapt this last paragraph to suit any particular situation.]

When you have finished, send some of all the love you have in your heart to someone who really needs it. See how good it makes them feel. Then feel the love coming back to you, even stronger than it was when you sent it out. Now take some of all that love you have in your heart and give it to yourself. Fill yourself up with love from your heart until you are filled with loving energy, from the tips of your toes to the top of your head... Now, whenever you're ready, you can open your eyes.

Chapter 5

Step Three:
Wishes, Dreams,
Goals and
Achievements

We all have wishes and dreams at some time. Some come true and some don't. When we make a commitment to manifesting a wish or a dream, it becomes a goal. Whenever we attain a goal our self-confidence receives an important and often permanent boost. Achieving goals is essential in the building of self-esteem.

The imagination is particularly influential when it comes to attaining a goal. The way we imagine will determine the level of our success both in terms of clarifying the goal and in terms of staying focused on it.

Understanding how powerful the imagination is can be a vital tool for children in their pursuit of dreams and goals. The younger they are when they learn to use imagery in a positive way, the simpler it will be for them. As they learn to focus their imagery skills to achieve what they want, their self-confidence and esteem will naturally increase.

Encouragement, demonstrating stick-to-it-iveness by example, and holding a loving, supporting space for your child(ren), are also important contributions you, as a parent or adult in the child's life, can make to support the attainment of their goals and to help their wishes and dreams come true.

A Story from Hawaii:

Holua-Manu

Long ago, soon after the Hawaiian people settled the island of Kauai, a man and a woman climbed a canyon and followed a stream that came to be known as Waimaka. Where two valleys joined the couple made their home. Fresh water flowed near their doorstep, bananas and taro grew wild, and fresh water shrimp were easy to catch. Best of all, they had a young son who was full of energy and flew from place to place, earning him the name of Manu, meaning bird.

Soon Manu's parents became lazy. They sat under the shade of a tree and watched Manu fly from place to place finding, preparing, cooking and serving the food they ate. Their bodies grew fatter and they moved less and less, but their eyes darted swiftly, searching for ways to amuse themselves.

The couple had two strange abilities. They were able to lift rocks into the air, move them about, and put them down in a new place, just by looking at them. They could also send freshets of water rushing down the stream bed at will. This lazy couple enjoyed dropping rocks near unwary strangers that came along the trail along Waimaka stream. Soon the strangers stopped coming into Waimaka, so the lazy parents sought their amusement by lifting stones and dropping them as close to their son as possible to see him jump with suspense and fear. Whenever Manu had to cross the stream, his parents sent down freshets to try to knock him off his feet. Their laughter would echo in the hills until it was time for them to eat. Then, the lazy parents shouted for Manu to bring the food he had found for them to eat. Whenever the food was slow in coming, Manu's father would complain, 'What use is a strong son, if he will not work for his parents?'

Manu flew from place to place

So Manu worked hard from morning till night.

Whenever Manu went to the stream to catch shrimp, he would pass by a water slide. It was a steep slope where people would throw themselves onto long narrow sleds and speed down the slide. Manu could think of nothing he would rather do than ride a sled down the water slide. There was never time to make a sled for himself, or to slide down the slide even if he had a sled, for there were always too many things he had to do to feed his parents. But at night, while his body slept, Manu would dream of flying down the water slide.

One evening, returning home with a bundle of taro, Manu, stumbled across a new water slide. As he stood looking at it in amazement, a tiny sled came hurtling down the slope. It hit a pebble and sped out into the air, tipping off the rider. Manu ran forward and caught the rider in mid-air, saving him from death on the rocks.

Manu set the little rider down with curiosity. The rider was hardly half as tall as Manu, a very small man with a curly brown beard. The little man darted off into the bushes so quickly that Manu was not sure where he had hidden. Manu smiled sadly for he would have liked to have someone to talk to about water sliding.

As he started homeward, he saw the tiny sled where it lay broken on some rocks. He picked it up and looked it over. 'Maybe I can fix it,' he murmured. And in fixing it, he thought, he could learn how to make one for himself. He strapped the sled to his back and trudged home.

In the days that followed, Manu found wood and shaped it to replace the broken cross pieces. When the sled was mended, he polished it until it gleamed.

Manu's parents were not happy. 'If you have time to make a sled,' they muttered, 'it shows what a lazy boy you are. Thinking only of yourself. How can you do this to us?'

'I have never ridden a sled,' Manu answered. 'I work from morning to evening. If only I could have a day to myself I would do nothing but slide down the water slide.'

'Then take a day off from work,' answered his parents. 'But first you must fill a large basket with food for us. And build a taro patch nearby, with fresh water flowing through it, so we can get taro if we want it. You must also plant some sugar cane and some bananas too. If you do this in the next three days, you may have one day all for yourself.'

'You are unkind to tease me,' protested Manu. 'You know I can't do all these things in three days.' His parents only laughed.

The next time Manu went to the place where he had caught the water slide rider, he took the little sled with him. He found the slide without trouble and placed the repaired sled where it could be easily seen. Then he continued on to search for food.

As he came back down the trail in the evening, the little bearded man appeared suddenly on the path in front of Manu, holding the repaired sled. 'I have come to thank you,' the little man said.

'I have done nothing,' answered Manu.

'You saved me from the rocks when I fell from my

sled,' the little man pointed out, 'And you repaired my sled. Truly you have done much.'

'No one has ever thanked me before,' said Manu in slow appreciation.

The little man asked, 'Why do you spend all day searching for food? Why don't you go sledding once in a while?'

'I would like nothing more,' Manu replied. 'But first I must make a taro patch near the river and then I must plant sugar cane and bananas.'

'Come sledding with me now,' urged the little man. 'There is a slide nearby, and my sled awaits you.'

'I cannot,' Manu said sadly. 'Your slide is too short for me and your sled could not carry my weight. I am already late and my parents will be angry.' He sighed deeply. 'But one day,' he said 'I will do what I would like to do. One day I will have put aside enough food for my parents and I will go sledding from sunrise to sunset.'

With that Manu walked home. As he had expected, his parents were angry and sent him out again to find shrimp. As he searched the stream his parents sent down a freshet which tumbled Manu in its rapids. The shouts of his parents' laughter echoed in the hills. But this time, unknown to Manu or his parents, other ears heard the laughter and were not amused.

During the night when Manu slept, the hum of a thousand tiny voices filled the air. As dawn came, the sound faded into the mountain ridges.

When Manu's parents awoke, they looked about them with astonishment. Beside their house was a taro patch with young taro plants nodding in the morning breeze. Sugar cane had been planted along the walls and banana plants grew in profusion. In front of the house there were many baskets filled with food.

Manu smiled. 'Now I can go water sliding,' he said. He went up to the little water slide to search for his friend, the little brown-bearded man.

'Where are you?' he called. 'Come out so that I can thank you.'

'No thanks necessary,' the little man said as he stepped out into the open. 'You saved my life.'

The little man led Manu to the top of the ridge. There, a long water slide had been made extending down the slope of the ridge, stretching right down into the stream sparkling far below them.

'Let us race!' the little man said. Grabbing his sled he ran for the slide, threw himself onto the sled and sped down the slope. Manu gently took the tall sled and followed him. At long last he found himself flying downhill with the ease of a bird and the speed of the wind.

His parents watched Manu angrily from under their tree. 'We must do something to stop Manu quickly,' his mother said. 'Otherwise he will never work for us again, but will stay there sledding all day long!'

They concentrated their powers, and as the two men climbed to the top of the ridge again, two great rocks rose in the air and came crashing down in the stream. As Manu flung himself onto the slide he saw the rocks and with great skill was able to jump high, skimming over the rocks and landing unhurt on the other side. His parents were even angrier to see how he avoided their obstacles. They sent a flood down the stream and Manu was tumbled about in the fierce water and his sled was smashed. The sound of his parents' laughter echoed in the valley.

Manu picked up his broken sled.

'Come now,' his father called. 'Work for us! You can never beat the floods we send.'

Manu came to where they sat. Quietly he said to them, 'For twenty years I have worked hard for you. I have worked day and night, always doing what you asked, as you yourselves did less and less. You have wasted the gifts the gods gave you, your power over rocks and water. You could have used your power to turn this whole valley into taro patches and keep them properly irrigated, giving us plenty of food right at hand. Instead, because you toss rocks and send freshets of water against visitors for your selfish amusement, no one comes and this valley is deserted and overgrown. And you have broken your promise to me. You promised me a day to myself in return for completing three tasks. The tasks were done, and yet you refuse to let me enjoy this day. I know now you will never be satisfied. Lead your own lives. I shall live mine.'

He picked up his sled and without glancing back climbed the ridge. His parents shouted at him but he didn't listen. They directed their powers to send a freshet of raging water over him, but this time the torrent did not come. They tried to throw rocks but the rocks did not move. The gods had taken back their gifts and the couple was now forced to work for themselves.

Manu repaired his sled and day after day he raced with the little men. His skill grew until he could ride his slide standing up. Manu's fame as a sled rider spread over the island and people came from every corner to watch him race and cheer his skill and daring. Manu's dream had finally come true.

A Story:

The Wishing Tree

Once upon a time there was a young man named Peter travelling through the forest. He was carrying a large rucksack on his back and he was travelling on foot. He had begun his travels at dawn and by dusk he was getting very tired. As he wondered whether he should rest he saw a large, beautiful tree by the side of the path.

'What a perfect place to sit down and rest,' he said to himself.

So Peter sat down, took off his rucksack and leaned against the trunk of the beautiful tree. As he relaxed he thought to himself, 'Boy, I am really hungry. I wish I had something to eat.' As soon as he had finished the thought, a large platter of food appeared in front of him. The platter was filled with all of Peter's favourite foods. He looked at it with amazement and thought to himself, 'Wow, I must have sat down under the famous wishing tree!'

Peter began to eat the food on the platter. Soon he

The wishing tree

had eaten everything and, leaning back against the tree, he thought, 'I wish I had something to drink.' With that a crate of his favourite drinks appeared before him.

Peter thought it was wonderful and immediately guzzled three drinks. He leaned back against the tree again and thought to himself, 'I could really use a nice big armchair.' Instantly an armchair appeared.

Peter was thrilled and sat down in the chair. After a while he thought to himself, 'Why, I'm under the wishing tree. I must be able to wish for whatever I want!' And he wished for chocolates. Suddenly there were chocolates everywhere! Next he wished for ice cream and all the ice cream he could possibly eat appeared before him. He kept on wishing for all the things he had ever wanted, until the sun set.

Then he thought to himself, 'Here I am alone in the middle of a large forest in the middle of the night. What if a wolf came along and ate me?'

And it did!

A Game:

Time Lines

You will need: paper and pencils.

Give each family member a sheet of paper and a pencil. Have each person draw a line that forks approximately half way across the page (see diagram below).

Along the horizontal line, ask each person to write down important things that have happened in their life. If they wish to keep their paper private, let them. The primary object of this game is self-awareness.

Along the top fork, ask everyone to write their ultimate dreams, wishes and goals for their future and along the bottom fork write what they believe to be their likely future.

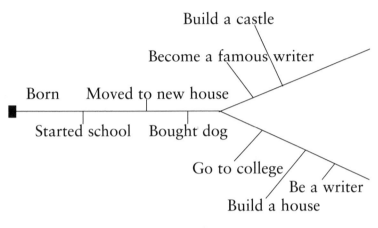

A time line

See how much difference there is between the likely future and the ultimate dreams, wishes and goals. Ask each other – or have everyone ask themselves – what you can do, or change, to make your dreams, wishes and goals more believable in your mind? What do you need to do, or change, to make your dreams, wishes and goals come true?

Have each person choose one thing they will do within a certain time period that can bring their wish closer. Discuss how you can all support each other. Then do it!

A Tool:

Treasure Album

You will need: a large scrap book each, scissors, glue, tape, colour pencils, magazine pictures and photos of yourselves.

Have each person create an album of pictures, poems, affirmations, photos and drawings depicting their *perfect future*. Use at least one page for each goal or dream, and make it as colourful and vivid as possible. Make sure that everyone has a few photos of themselves that they can cut out and glue onto the perfect picture.

The treasure album can be designed as a comic book, a treasure map, a photo album, an illustrated story book, or whatever you like. Let the imagination take over! No limits! Encourage everyone (including yourself) to make their album come alive. For example, put a few drops of scent relative to a goal on that page – i.e. ginger perfume oil on a page showing your goal of travelling to a Pacific island.

Remember, you are putting together *the end result*, not *how* you are going to achieve it.

This can easily be an ongoing family project and can help you all stay focused on your goals, and increase the enjoyment of reaching them.

<u>A Tool:</u>

A 'Personal Plan' Tree

You will need: paper and pencils.

At the top of the page write _____ 'S PLAN.

Fill in your name on the line. Draw a box in the centre of the page and write your ultimate goal in the box. Put the pencil down for a moment, close your eyes and be still. Take your attention down to your heart. Holding your attention there, think of something that makes you feel good, and that brings a warm, loving feeling to your heart. Focus on that for a moment, until you feel like you might want to smile. Hold that feeling, open your eyes, pick up the pencil and see how many ideas your heart comes up with to help you achieve your goal. Write your ideas as branches from a 'tree' of your ultimate goal. Make connections between the ideas. Write down everything that comes to mind, no matter how strange it may seem. Fill the page if you want and, as you write, watch your own personal plan unfold! (See the example diagram.)

<u>A Visualization:</u>

Your Theatre

Guide your child(ren) in the same way as described in Chapter 3, p. 33.

GOAL: Give a Speech

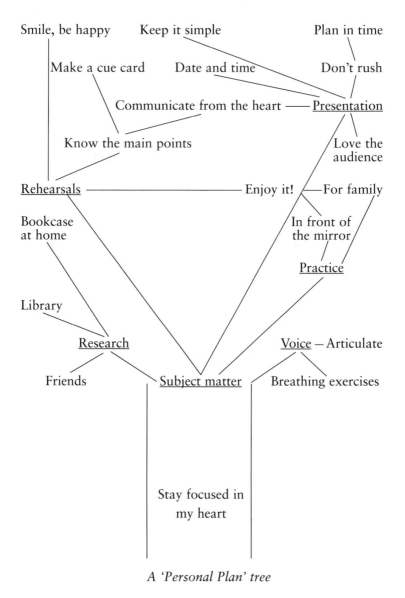

A 'Personal Plan' tree

Relax and close your eyes. Breathe deeply and evenly. [You may want to breathe deeply and slowly a few times with your child. This helps the relaxation process.] *Now focus all your attention on your heart and think of something you love. ... Enjoy how that makes you feel ... Now see before you a large theatre. It is situated in the most perfect place and is designed exactly the way you like it ... Now go into the theatre through the front entrance or the stage door, whichever you prefer. This is your theatre. Wander through it for a while, exploring it ... Notice any particular colours, any special sounds, any smells ... What is the temperature like? ... Feel the peace and quiet of your theatre ... Now go into the auditorium and sit down on one of the seats near the centre ... Feel the texture of the material on the seat. Make yourself comfortable ...*

On the seat next to you is a glossy brochure. You pick it up and look at it. The brochure describes your goal very accurately and in full-page colour photos! ... There are many photos in the brochure, each one equally descriptive of your goal. Take some time to look at each photo. Notice all the details and enjoy your brochure. [long pause] *You hear a noise now and look up. A director is walking onto the stage from the wings. It is your very own director and can therefore be whoever you want ... Your director begins to speak, telling you about practice/rehearsals ... explaining what needs to be done before your goal can be attained ... Listen to your director ...* [pause] *... Now your*

director leaves the stage and the lights dim. One
large spotlight hits centre stage – and in it is you!
... Your play begins. It is the attainment of your
goal being performed before your very eyes. Watch
and enjoy it ... [pause] Your play is complete and
the curtain closes. You thank your director and the
entire cast of players, knowing they will all be there
for you whenever you need them. You thank your
theatre. You leave your theatre now, knowing that
you can achieve the goal you have set for yourself
... Bring your attention now back into your heart.
Take some of all that love you have there and send
it to all the people in your play. See the love
beaming out from your heart to theirs. See it come
back to you even stronger than it was when you
sent it out. Feel how good it makes you feel. Feel
yourself filling up with love from your heart until
you are filled with loving energy from the tips of
your toes to the top of your head. Feel all that
energy in your body ... and whenever you are
ready you can open your eyes.

You can enhance the effect of this visualization by
suggesting that your child imagine the attainment of
her goal – rekindling the *feeling* they had when
'seeing' it in their visualization – whenever
performing any task or step *towards* their goal.

Chapter 6

Step Four: Fulfilment and Appreciation

Recently, scientific studies have been carried out researching the power and significance of the heart and feelings of appreciation, love, care, compassion, forgiveness, humour, etc.* Strong connections have been made between the levels and frequencies of these feelings and our capacity for self-healing and stress management. The effect on the body of the various feelings associated with love has been shown to vary in strength. Scientific studies have actually measured the strength and power of the different feelings. The findings of these studies show that – of all the feelings we experience or thoughts we have that lead to these feelings – the feeling of *appreciation* is one of the most powerful and has one of the most positive effects on the body.

Personal fulfilment – something I believe all of us would like to see our children experience and which

---

*Scientific studies carried out by the Institute of HeartMath: see p. 110 for contact details.

is imperative in creating *sustained* self-esteem – is difficult to achieve without the feeling of appreciation: appreciation for all that is in our lives, appreciation for who we are, appreciation for where we are, appreciation for our personal achievements and appreciation for all that gives us fulfilment.

As science has now demonstrated the immense power of appreciation, I believe this is one of the greatest gifts we can give our children: the understanding and experience of *sincere appreciation* (as opposed to the command to 'show gratitude!').

<u>A Story from China:</u>

The Stonecutter

Once upon a time, many, many years ago in ancient China, there lived a stonecutter. He was a very angry and bitter man, always complaining about his bad luck.

On day, as he walked past the mansion of a rich merchant, he began muttering his usual complaints. 'What a wonderful and powerful man that merchant is,' he thought. 'I wish I could be like him. If I were like him, then I wouldn't have to spend all my time cutting and shaping stone!'

Suddenly, to his great amazement, he found himself transformed into a rich merchant. He had great power and wealth and was surrounded by luxury. One day he was lounging in his sedan chair looking up at the sky above him. He watched the sun shining high up in the sky, completely unaffected by anything. 'How proud the sun is,' he thought. 'If only I were the sun, then nothing could stop me from being still, peaceful and content.'

At that very moment the man was transformed into the sun. He shone down brightly into the countryside. Soon a large dark grey cloud moved between himself and the earth, so that his light could no longer reach the countryside below. 'How powerful that cloud is,' he thought. 'If only I were that cloud. Then I wouldn't be outdone by anything else!'

Immediately he was transformed into a rain cloud. He took great pleasure in causing floods all over the country. One day a strong wind came along and blew him all over the place. 'How very forceful the wind is,' he thought. 'If only I were the wind. Then I could really have my own way!'

Sure enough he was transformed into the wind. He roared and he raged and he blew things all over the place. One day he came across one thing that he could not move, no matter how hard he blew. It was a giant rock. 'How sturdy that rock is,' he thought. 'If only I could be that rock. Then nothing would ever have any impact on me!'

Instantly he was transformed into a giant rock. He felt very powerful and completely unmovable. Suddenly he heard a knocking. It was the knock, knock, knock of a hammer hitting a chisel. All at once he realized that he was being chipped away at. 'How could there be something more powerful than a giant rock?' he thought. He looked down to where

No matter how hard he blew ...

the sound was coming from. There, at the very base
of the rock, was a man with a hammer and chisel,
chipping, shaving and carving.

It was a stonecutter.

<u>A Story from England:</u>

The Young Oak Tree

Once upon a time there were two oak trees in a meadow somewhere in England, an old oak tree that had stood there for many years and was large and sturdy and a new, young oak tree that was small and quite frail.

The young oak tree wasn't very happy. 'Please Old Oak,' he cried, 'please don't make me push my roots down any further. It's so damp and cold in the earth and I keep bumping into rocks!' The young oak was on the verge of tears.

'Now, now,' said the old oak. 'Soon it'll be springtime and there will be spring winds. Then it'll be summertime and summer storms. Your roots have to be strong to keep the rest of you in place. And your roots must be deep in the earth so that they can find nourishing food to feed you, to make your trunk and branches and leaves strong and healthy.'

'Oh all right!' sighed the young oak.

'Don't worry,' said the old oak encouragingly. 'By next spring you will have grown so tall and strong, you'll be amazed!'

So the young oak continued to push his roots deeper and deeper into the ground, until spring.

One spring morning when the sun was shining, the young oak tree happened to glance across at his branches, and lo and behold, there were the most beautiful green buds all over them! The young oak tree thought they were wonderful. He felt so handsome and proud ... until one day he felt his buds about to burst. He was devastated.

'Old Oak!' he cried. 'Look at my branches and my beautiful buds. They are about to burst. What shall I do?'

'There, there, Young Oak,' said the old oak in a comforting voice. 'Don't panic. You're not losing anything. Have patience and you'll be pleasantly surprised.'

'But how can you be sure of that?' asked the young oak.

'You will learn that when you let go of something, it will always be replaced by something better.'

The young oak trusted the wisdom of the old oak, so he let go. And almost as soon as he did, hundreds of tiny leaves began to appear all over the young oak's branches.

'Look at me!' squealed the young oak with delight. 'I'm even more beautiful. You were right!'

As spring turned into summer the young oak became more and more beautiful. Many families of birds built nests in his branches and lived happily there, which made the young oak happy as well. He was happy that he was strong and healthy with deep roots and that he was able to share his beautiful leaves with others.

One day he noticed that little brown seeds were beginning to form. The old oak told him they were acorns and the young oak was happy with them as well. But then they started to fall off, and the young oak also noticed that his leaves were beginning to change colour. He was not happy at all!

Hundreds of tiny leaves appeared

'Old Oak!' he cried. 'What is happening to me? My acorns are falling off and my leaves are changing colour!'

'Remember what I told you in the spring,' the old oak said. 'Whenever you let go of something, it will be replaced by something better. You see, when you let go of something, you are giving it away and sharing it. When you lose all your acorns, they will be gathered up by squirrels who will store them for food for the winter. A few acorns will fall into warm cracks in the earth, and when spring comes they will sprout roots and begin to grow – just like you did!'

The young oak was silent, listening to the old oak. 'When autumn comes,' continued the old oak 'you will discover that your leaves have turned into beautiful shades of orange, gold and red. Then, when winter comes, all your leaves will fall off completely.'

'All my leaves will fall off?' exclaimed the young oak. 'But that will make me ugly, and then I'll never be wise and old like you!'

'Ah, but you will!' replied the old oak, 'because that is exactly how I became wise and strong.'

The young oak was very puzzled and wondered if he would ever understand what the old oak meant. But as time passed he began to understand. He watched as his acorns fell to the ground and the little squirrels gathered them up for winter food. He watched as his leaves turned orange and gold and red and then began to fall as well. He watched as children played in his fallen leaves, laughing and frolicking, and he was suddenly quite happy to share them. When winter arrived, the young oak was so glad he had shared himself he didn't mind being ugly for a while; after all, he had springtime to look forward to. Then his roots would be longer, his branches would reach higher, his leaves would be bigger, his trunk would be stronger and he would be older and wiser … like Old Oak.

<u>A Game:</u>

Collage

You'll need: a large sheet of paper, photos, magazine pictures, scissors and glue.

Find pictures of things that make you happy and that help you go to your heart. Cut them out and paste them, in a collage, on the sheet of paper. Hang it up somewhere visible, where you pass frequently, to help you remember to stay in your heart and feel appreciation.

Each family member can make their own collage and you can also make a combined family collage and hang it up in the kitchen.

<u>A Tool:</u>

100 Blessings

You'll need: paper and pencils.

Each person needs a piece of paper and a pencil. During the course of one day, or several if necessary, each person writes down 100 things they appreciate about their life. Share one of these things with the family at the next meal you have together. Continue to do this for the next 100 days. (Keep adding things to your list and you'll never run out of appreciation to share!)

A Tool:

Gift

You'll need: paper and colour pencils.

Divide up into pairs. Each person draws a gift they would like to give to their partner. When everyone has finished drawing, swap drawings and guess why your partner would like you to have that specific gift. Share your thoughts and exchanges with the whole family.

A Visualization:

Heart Mail

As in the other visualizations, be sure you and your child(ren) are in a calm, relaxed state of mind and body. Read this slowly and audibly, pausing frequently.

Close your eyes and breathe deeply a few times, relaxing all over ... Now bring your attention to your heart. Feel all the energy in your feet and legs move up to your heart ... Now feel all the energy in your hips and stomach move up to your heart ... Feel the energy in your hands, arms and shoulders move in to your heart. Feel the energy in your head, face, neck and chest move down to your heart, until all of your body is completely relaxed and all your energy is in your heart. Imagine breathing the energy in and out through your heart ... [pause] As you breathe, think of something or someone you really appreciate. Now send some of all the love you have in your heart to that person. See the love and appreciation pouring out of your heart and filling up that person. Keep sending love and appreciation and see it coming back to you even stronger than it was when you began sending it.

Feel yourself filling up with love. Now appreciate yourself for having so much love and appreciation, and appreciate your body for working so well and your mind for working so well. Try to feel this appreciation and love in every part of your body and feel yourself filling up with loving energy ... feel it from the bottom of your toes to the top of your head ... Whenever you are ready, you can open your eyes.

Chapter 7

Step Five: Family and Relationship Dynamics

Family dynamics play a vital role in how we experience relationships – with others and with ourselves. Our family dynamics, relationships and values are at the very core of our sense of self and how we experience ourselves in interaction with others. However, the concept of family has changed considerably and in most cases is not the same for children today as it was for their parents when they were growing up. Family structures have changed: according to recent statistics, 6.6 million children in the United States live with divorced single parents and 7.6 million children are in step families. *Time* has become very limited: 61 per cent of children live in families in which both parents work outside the home (by the year 2000 the figure will be 80 per cent), and over 20 per cent of children in the United States, ages 6–12, haven't had a 10 minute conversation with a parent in a month. Family values have become difficult to uphold and often even to establish in the first place! As adults, we are frequently so busy involving ourselves in social, professional and world politics that we neglect to involve ourselves sufficiently in the politics of our own family. Our children, however, are much more interested in the politics of their families than in the politics of the Middle East, their own country, or even their own community. Since the individual and the family are, in very many ways, microcosms of the greater society, it may be beneficial to our society if we spend more time on, and give more priority to, developing creative, non-violent communication and problem-solving skills within the family.

By finding ways to avoid verbal and physical violence, 'put-downs' and hurtful interactions at the basic family level, and by developing creative, loving alternatives, we can affect our children, their current and future relationships, and our society in very important ways.

The following story has no ending by design. The idea is that you, as a family, design or write your own ending. Have each family member write their own, and/or write one together. Share ideas and explore the questions at the end of the story.

A Story:

The Large and Beautiful Palace

Once upon a time there lived a king who built a large and beautiful palace. He had four children and he gave the palace to all of them to live in.

The first brother to arrive at the palace moved into all the upstairs rooms. The first sister to arrive at the palace moved into all the downstairs rooms. The two spent most of their time arguing and fighting, because each one wanted to be in charge of the whole palace. When the second brother and sister arrived there were no rooms left in the palace for them to live in.

'As I am very kind,' said the first brother to the second brother, 'I will give you one of my very own rooms if you will do all the work in the fields, growing all the food.'

'I too am very kind,' said the first sister to the second sister. 'I will give you one of my very own rooms if you will do all the cooking and washing and cleaning.'

The large and beautiful palace

Of course, the rooms they offered were the smallest and least beautiful of the many rooms in the large and beautiful palace. But the second brother and sister had no choice but to accept them if they wanted a roof over their heads. So they worked all day long from dawn until dusk, growing the food, cooking, washing and cleaning. They both knew that this was not what their father had in mind when he built the large and beautiful palace, because he loved all his children equally. But their work was so hard that they were too tired and worn out to complain to their brother and sister.

When the first brother noticed that the second brother became ill from overwork he said, 'I will give you medicine to make you better. I know father will be pleased with me for my kindness.'

When the first sister noticed that the second sister was cold because her clothes had become thin and worn out, she said 'I will give you my black coat that has become too tight for me. I know father will be pleased with me for my kindness.'

Then, one day, when nobody was expecting him, the king arrived at the palace to visit his children …

Before you make up your ending(s) to this story, it may help to ask yourself the following questions:

Have you ever been treated unfairly?
How did you feel?
How fair are brothers and sisters?

Do people who do unfair things know they are
being unfair?
If not, why don't they know?
Do you know anyone who is unfairly treated?
What can be done to put things right?

<u>Your Story:</u>

Attention Parents!

Tell a story about your own childhood or about other
family members. Keep it light and humorous if
possible, to start with. Do not use your story to make
a point or to preach or lecture. The purpose is to give
your children a stronger sense of family and of
connection to you and to who you are.

<u>A Game:</u>

The Talking Stick

You'll need: a wooden stick, preferably from nature,
that doesn't give splinters and is pleasant to hold.

Sit in a circle. One person holds the talking stick and
says 'One thing I like about my family is ...' or 'One
good thing the family did this week is ...' or
'Something fun I remember about our family is ...'.

When this person has finished sharing their 'good family thing', he or she passes the talking stick on to the person on his or her left. The talking stick continues being passed around the circle in this manner until everyone has shared 'one good family thing'.

This game is called the Talking Stick because only the person holding the stick is allowed to talk!

You can take this game further by sending the talking stick around a second time, but this time have each person share 'One thing that upset me this week was ...'. If this is done, it is important that:

- nobody interrupts,
- the word YOU is preferably not used by the speaker,
- nobody responds to anything said by anyone else.

This is a game for airing and sharing only.

When the talking stick has come full circle, it may be a good idea to do one more round, saying 'What I could do to make myself feel better ...' or 'What I could do to make the family feel better ...'.

This game can be used effectively to resolve disputes. It is, however, important that *only the person holding the talking stick can talk*. A time limit for speaking may be appropriate. Should a family member not wish to speak, it is OK to say 'Pass'!

A Visualization:

Heart to Heart

If there is someone in your family you would like to help, or someone you are having a problem with that you don't quite know what to do about, the following may help you both feel better!

Sit in a quiet place, either side by side or opposite each other, or you *can* do this alone. You may wish to record the following script on a cassette in advance.

> *Close your eyes and relax your body. As you breathe calmly, imagine your body sinking into the surface beneath you until you are completely relaxed. Now take your attention to your heart and to the area around your heart. Feel the rhythm of your heartbeat. Listen closely and see if you can feel a peace, a stillness, deep inside of you. Think of anything that makes you feel peaceful ... [pause] Feel the peace within your heart. Hold that feeling in your heart ... Now send some of the peacefulness in your heart to the other person. Feel yourself sending out that peaceful, calm feeling from your heart and imagine the other person becoming more and more peaceful and content as they receive peace from your heart ... [pause] Now see if you can feel their appreciation for this peace. Keep holding onto that feeling of peace within you, and keep sending peace to the other person ... Finally, send some peace around yourself and fill the room up with peace before you open your eyes.*

<u>A Tool:</u>

Heart-to-Heart Listening

Divide up into pairs and sit down facing each other. Take a moment to close your eyes and focus your attention on your heart and on anything that makes you feel love, peace or appreciation. Just hold that feeling in your hearts for a moment. Then open your eyes and try to keep the feeling alive in your hearts. (Some soft music in the background that you *all* love may help.)

Have one person in each pair say the following to their partner:

> *I invite you to speak, for three minutes, about anything you like. I promise to stay in my heart and to listen with all my attention, from my heart. I also promise that I will not comment on what you say other than to feed back to you the essence of what you said, after you have finished. I promise that I will not raise this issue again in the near future [i.e. within the next week] unless you invite me to.*

It is important that the listener fully intends to keep these promises, as it allows him or her to *really* listen, without their own agenda or thoughts of 'comeback' getting in the way. This in turn allows the speaker to really feel listened to and can often, in itself, resolve issues, problems or disagreements without any further discussion or input from anyone else, including the listener!

The feeding back of the *essence* of what was said, by the listener, is important only in that it allows the speaker to know that he was fully heard.

The more you practise using this tool while *being in the heart*, the easier and more effective you will find it.

Chapter 8

Step Six:
Community –
Self-Care and
Other-Care

This chapter is an extension of the previous one, having the approach that your community, ideally, can be an *extended* family, creating a strong support system for your family and for your child(ren). As such, your community, or your child's community, can consist of your greater family, your friends, your child's class and school, your colleagues, your neighbourhood or the town you live in. In Hawaii, there is a word for the extended family and for the *feeling* it creates – Ohana.

A strong sense of Ohana and community is a most valuable asset to any child and to his ability to contribute and share his unique talents with self-confidence and with love. I believe it is a vital component for the future of the human race.

A Story:

The Prophecy

Once upon a time there was a small community of people who were not getting along with each other at all. They would bicker and argue and fight all day and all night. Finally, everyone became so disgruntled they began to think of disbanding the whole community altogether!

Then one night their minister had a vision. The vision was very simple and very short. The vision told him, 'One of your members is the Messiah.'

The minister shared his vision with the rest of the community and from that day on things began to change.

Every day when one member of the community was with another member they would think, 'Maybe this is the Messiah.' So they began to treat one another with more love, with more care and with more respect. When each member of the community got up in the morning and looked in the mirror they would think, 'Maybe I am the one, Maybe I am the Messiah.' So they began to treat themselves with more love, with more care and with more respect.

And so the community began to prosper. None of the members bickered or argued or fought any more. Soon the community began to grow. People from far and wide came to join the community and it became known for the love, care and respect that flourished there. So it was that the community that had been dying came to thrive!

They began to treat one another with love

<u>A Story:</u>

Chopsticks

Once upon a time there lived a woman who had worked all her life to bring about good in the world. As she lay on her deathbed she was told by an angel that she could make one wish, as a reward for all her good deeds. Her wish was to visit both heaven and hell before died. Her wish was granted.

All at once she was whisked off to a great banqueting hall. The tables were piled high with delicious food and drink of every imaginable kind. Around the tables sat miserable looking, starving people as wretched as could be.

'Why are the people like this?' she asked the angel.

'Look at their arms,' the angel replied.

She looked and saw that attached to the people's arms were chopsticks secured above their elbows. These were so long that the wretched people could

Chopsticks

not place the delicious food in their mouths, and so they remained hungry, frustrated and utterly miserable.

'Indeed, this is hell!' the woman exclaimed. 'Take me away from here!' She was then whisked off to heaven.

Again she found herself in a great banqueting hall with tables piled high with food and drink of every imaginable kind. Around the tables sat people laughing, contented and joyful.

'No chopsticks, I suppose?' she asked the angel.

'Oh yes there are,' replied the angel. 'Look – just as in hell they are long and attached above the elbow. But look closer.' The woman looked at the happy, laughing people. 'Here,' the angel continued, 'the people have learnt to feed one another.'

A Game:

Three's a Team

You'll need: a marshmallow, candy or piece of dried fruit and some string.

Suspend your treat by the string, from the ceiling. Make sure it is suspended about a foot above the head of the tallest person in the room. Elect three people and tell them that they can have the treat if they can get it down without touching it, or the string, with their hands.

They will eventually discover that the only way to do this is for two people to lift one person and for that person to take the treat in his or her mouth. Once it has been in the mouth of that person, he or she can do little else but eat it! Discuss what this implies.

A Game:

If I Were a Colour

You'll need: paper and pencils.

Give everybody a sheet of paper with the following list on it. Ask each person to fill in the blanks. Afterwards, share some of your choices, the reasons why you made them and how you feel about your own and each other's choices. Use the Talking Stick (p. 80) to help ensure that everybody gets to share equally.

If I were a colour I'd be __

If I were an animal I'd be a __

If I were a fish I'd be a __

If I were a bird I'd be a __

If I were a vegetable I'd be a __

If I were a fruit I'd be a __

If I were a tree I'd be a __

If I were a town I'd be a __

If I were a country I'd be __

If I were a song I'd be __

If I were a dance I'd be __

If I were an instrument I'd be __

A Visualization:

Future Image

Before you begin, discuss the meaning of community. What is your community like? Your community might be your family, friends, class, school, neighbourhood or town. Try to think of one thing about your community that makes you feel good, one thing that helps you stay in your heart.

Now, guide your family through this visualization. You might like to pre-record it so that you too can participate. Refer to guidelines for previous creative visualizations (p. 33).

Imagine for a moment that you are somewhere where you feel at peace. Choose the place you want to be in. What can you see? What can you feel? ... Imagine that you can see in the distance a path that leads up to a hillside. Imagine you are walking along this path. There are fields on either side of you and the sun is shining. You can hear birds and insects around you. The sun shines through the leaves and branches make patterns of light and shadow on the ground in front of you. Walk along a little further until you see a sign.

The sign says COMMUNITY OF THE FUTURE. Follow the path until you see the community in the distance. You approach the buildings that house the community. It is some time in the twenty-first century; the community has been working for many years on love, peace and living from the heart. It is an ideal community. You decide to visit.

See the children, women and men living and working together here. What do you see? ... You enter one of the buildings. What do you hear? ... What do you smell? ... What else do you see? ... Touch a few things. Look at the children. What are they doing? ... Can you see their faces? Watch the children as you wander through the community. Have a good look around and see what it's like in this place. What are you feeling now? What is the most important thing you see? ...

Have a final look around before you leave. Now go into your heart and just feel your own breathing for a moment ... Stay in your heart and focus on the feeling of appreciation ... Now, as soon as you're ready, you can open your eyes.

Write down, draw and share with each other what you saw. When you share, use the Talking Stick (see p. 80). What was the same as it is now and what was different? How can you all create more of what you want? Take plenty of time writing and drawing your images and the responses to these questions – and any other thoughts you might have. The more you and your children focus on your ideal, the more likely it is to happen!

Chapter 9

Step Seven: The Earth – Global Awareness

Increasing global awareness and a sense of responsibility for the planet we inhabit is more important now than ever before. Most children today are very aware of this, and of a need to experience their relationship to *all* creation, to feel part of a greater whole.

When a strong sense of *self, self-care* and *self-confidence* is developed – with an ensuing sense of family and community – there follows a *natural* progression to genuine and sustained global awareness and environmental care.

A Story from Indonesia:

Heart of Gold

Once upon a time there lived a man who was so rich that his wealth filled up all the storehouses of his large palace and even spilled out into the grounds.

The one thing he enjoyed most of all was giving away his belongings to the poor. Every afternoon he brought baskets full of food, clothing and fine things into the grounds of his palace and gave them away. He was known far and wide as Heart of Gold.

One day Shakra, one of the gods, came to hear of Heart of Gold's generosity and decided to set him a test. 'It is easy for a rich man to be generous,' he said. 'Let him lose some of his wealth, then we shall see if his heart is truly made of gold!'

That very night, Shakra caused all the fine ornaments, jewellery and beautiful clothes to disappear from Heart of Gold's palace. But when Heart of Gold woke up in the morning he wasn't at all bothered. So Shakra decided to set him a harder test. Next morning when Heart of Gold woke up, he

Heart of Gold

found his palace completely empty. All that was left was a rope, a sickle and the nightshirt he was wearing.

Heart of Gold took the rope and the sickle and went out into the fields to work. All day long he worked in the hot sun, thinking only of earning enough pennies to give to those that were poorer than himself.

Then the god Shakra appeared to him and said, 'Foolish man, why do you not work to save up your money until you are rich again? There is nothing wrong in not giving when you have so little.'

Heart of Gold replied, 'Shakra, if a poor man asks for my help today, I cannot ask him to wait until I am rich again. I will not change my practice of charity. Giving brings comfort to others and great joy to me.'

Then the god Shakra saw that his heart was truly made of gold, and with a wave of his hand he restored all Heart of Gold's fine possessions and riches to him. Heart of Gold continued generously to give away his things to the poor and the sick.

A Story from India:

The Banyan Tree

In India there is a big tree called the banyan tree. It grows in the forest and many animals make their homes there.

Once upon a time there was a particularly large

banyan tree growing in a forest and many different animals had made it their home. One day a man came along with a big axe. He stopped at the tree, looked at it and said, 'What a big tree! I can cut this tree down and sell the wood at the market. With all the money I'll make I will be able to buy land and build a big house. I'll be able to buy sheep and goats and get myself a wife.'

When the animals heard this they came out of their homes in the tree. First of all four little mice appeared. They said to the man, 'Please don't cut the tree down. We live under the roots of the tree. It is our home and our shelter.'

The banyan tree

Then some moths and beetles came to speak to the man with the axe. They said, 'Please don't cut the tree down. We live in the bark of the tree. It is our home and our shelter.'

Next a swarm of bees flew down to speak the man. They said, 'Please don't cut the tree down. We live inside the trunk of the tree. It is our home and our shelter.'

Then a family of monkeys came to speak to the man. They said, 'Please don't cut down the tree. We live in the branches of the tree. It is our home and our shelter.'

Last of all, the birds came to speak to the man with the axe. They said, 'Please don't cut the tree down. We live among the leaves of the tree. It is our home and our shelter.'

The man with the axe waved his hand with an impatient gesture. He said, 'I haven't got time to listen to you! I want to cut the tree down. Go away! Shoo!'

The animals became very angry. The birds began to peck at the man's hair. He shouted, 'Ouch! Stop it! That hurts!' But he wouldn't put down his axe. The monkeys threw fruit at him. He shouted, 'Ouch! Stop it! That hurts!' But still he wouldn't put down his axe. The beetles and moths flew in his face. He shouted, 'Ouch! Stop it! That hurts!' But he held onto his axe. The bees stung his hands. The man shouted, 'Ouch! Stop it! That hurts!' And then he became scared. So scared was the man of the animals, he ran away as fast as he could!

The little mice hadn't been able to do anything to

scare the man with the axe, but they thanked all the other animals. To this day, all the animals live happily in the very big banyan tree and it is still their home and their shelter.

A Game:

Webbing

You'll need: coloured wool or string. Paper, glue and pencils.

Ask your family to sit on the floor, in a circle. Have one person hold the ball of wool and stand near the edge of the circle. Imagine that you are all in a position to create a brand new planet. Think of what you would put on this planet. Begin with nature, for example, 'trees'. Whoever suggests the first thing takes the end of the wool. Think of other things, for example, 'grass' or 'flowers'. Whoever suggests the second thing holds the wool further along. Move on to other elements such as plants, vegetables, water, soil, animals and so on, connecting people with the wool as their relationships to the rest of the group emerge. Continue in this way until the entire family is strung together in a symbol of the web of life.

Then begin demonstrating how each individual is important to the entire community by taking away one member of the web – i.e. the trees get chopped down. In this example, the person representing 'trees' will tug on the wool. Any other person who feels the tug will also yank the wool, and people who feel the second tug will tug likewise. In this way it is tangibly demonstrated that *everything* is affected by the death of trees.

When you have finished this game, let everyone share their thoughts and experiences. Then have everyone take a piece of wool, a sheet of paper and a pencil, and make their own web by gluing their wool onto the paper and drawing around it all that they would create on 'their planet' or their web of life.

A Game:

Leaves

You'll need: a pile of leaves from the same tree.

Ask everyone to take one leaf each, any leaf they choose. Let each person look closely and carefully at his leaf, smell it, feel the texture and the weight, and get acquainted with the uniqueness of that leaf. Then ask everyone to place their leaf back in the pile and to close their eyes. Mix up all the leaves. Ask everyone to open their eyes and find their leaf in the pile.

Let everyone share their experience and what they think we can learn from this about people and about living things on the earth.

A Visualization and Activity:

The Earth

Read the guidelines for creative visualizations (see p. 33) before you guide your family through the following process.

Breathe deeply and evenly and gently close your eyes. Feel all the muscles in your face relax. Bring all your attention to your heart and imagine breathing in and out through your heart. Focus on something simple that you really appreciate – a flower, a pet or a pleasant memory. Enjoy the feeling of appreciation for a moment.

Now see before you a plant, any plant. Notice how green the leaves are. Feel the texture of the leaves and smell their scent ... Focus your attention on your heart again and the feeling of appreciation, then appreciate your plant and how beautiful it is. Enjoy the feeling these thoughts give you ... Now feel yourself gradually begin to grow smaller ... smaller and smaller, smaller and smaller, until you can sit on one of the leaves of your plant. How does the leaf feel now? ... Begin to slide down the leaf, hold onto the stalk and slowly slide down the stalk, getting smaller and smaller, until you land on the earth and are merely the size of a small particle of earth ... You are now part of the earth. Feel yourself going into the earth, you are one with the earth. Feel the temperature, the texture, the smell ... Feel the soil and the rocks and the clay and every particle of earth as part of you ... [pause]. A spade is now gently digging around the base of the plant. Feel yourself and the soil around you being shifted. The roots of the plant are loosening underneath you ... You are lifted up on the spade together with the plant and all the earth, and you are placed in new earth. Feel yourself blending with the new soil, being gently tossed about, and then watered. You become moist and cool. You are settling in now. Enjoy it ... Now gradually come up out of the earth, up along the stalk and up onto the leaf – gradually return to your normal self and size. Appreciate the plant and the earth and feel the love you have in your heart for them, knowing now that you are one with them both. Thank them for being there for you.

Now take your attention back into your heart and spread some of all that love you have there, all around your body. Feel the energy from your heart spread all the way down into your toes and all the way out to the tips of your fingers and up to the top of your head. Become aware of the surface beneath you and the room around you. As soon as you are ready you can open your eyes.

Invite everybody to share their experiences. Follow this with an outdoor activity such as re-potting a plant, planting plants in the garden or just digging. See whether this visualization has heightened the senses and the awareness of the earth and all that grows there.

A Visualization:

Planet Heart

Remember the guidelines for creative visualization (see p. 33) when guiding your family through this process.

Have your family sit or lie in a quiet place and relax for a moment. You can also do this while you're in the car, in bed, or anywhere your children can be quiet for a moment.

Imagine a stream of light going into your heart. Feel your heart filling up with light and love. Now feel the light filling up your body until you are entirely filled up with light and love. Now feel the area around you filling up, and the room (or car) around you. The light is filling up the building (or road) you are in, the town, the county and then the whole country. Feel the light streaming through your heart, filling the whole world, covering the whole planet with light and love ...

Now feel yourself growing larger and larger, and the world becoming smaller and smaller ... Soon you are so large that you find yourself floating above the earth. Compared to you, the earth is now the size of a balloon. The light is still streaming through your heart. Send some of all that love you have in your heart to the people and creatures on planet earth. Send it everywhere so everyone feels they are bathing in bright, loving sunlight. See all the people and the creatures turn their faces towards the loving sunlight and see them all feeling the peace and love you are sending ...

Feel the love and peace coming back to you from them. Enjoy it ... Now gradually return to your normal size, still feeling the love and peace in your heart. Know now that you can FILL the world with the love in your heart.

Finding
More
Tools

I hope the tools in this book have helped you – as they have helped me – explore and expand your vocabulary to become a more empowered parent, with more empowered children.

You may have found that some tools work better for you than others – that stories work better than games, or visualizations are more powerful than stories – and you may want to find more of the tools that work for you and for your children. Although you will probably have to do a little searching, you *can* find a multitude of resources that support creative parenting and the building of self-esteem in children.

Your local library is always a good place to start, as are secondhand book stores, alternative and health food stores that stock books, and alternative educational organizations. You will find a list of useful addresses at the back of this book as well as a resource list and recommended further reading.

Albert Einstein once said that 'imagination is more

important than knowledge'. In my experience, this approach is a powerful tool for parenting and for supporting children as they grow and build their self-esteem. I would like to add, however, that *parenting from the heart* is the most important tool of all; when a child feels truly loved, the very foundation for building self-esteem has been laid.

Recommended Further Reading

Bettelheim, Bruno, *A Good Enough Parent*, Pan Books, London, 1988

Campion, Mukti Jain, *The Good Parent Guide*, Element Books, Shaftesbury, 1993

Carey, Ken, *Notes to my Children*, Uni Sun, Kansas City, Missouri, 1984

Childre, Doc Lew, *A Parenting Manual*, Planetary Publications, Boulder Creek, CA, 1995

Childre, Doc Lew, *Teaching Children to Love*. Boulder Creek, CA, Planetary Publications, Boulder Creek, 1996

Cornell, J. *Sharing Nature with Children*, Exley Publications, Watford, Herts, 1989

Dale, Stan, *My Child, My Self: How to Raise the Child You Always Wanted To Be*, Human Awareness Publications, San Mateo CA, 1992

Day, Jennifer, *Creative Visualization with Children: A Practical Guide*, Element Books, Shaftesbury, 1994

Dyer, Wayne W. *What Do You Really Want For Your Children? How To Raise Healthy And Happy Kids*, Bantam Books, New York, 1985

Eyre, Linda and Richard, *Teaching Children Joy*, Ballantine Books, New York, 1980

Recommended Further Reading

Fontana, David, *Growing Together: Parent-Child Relationships as a Path to Wholeness and Happiness*, Element Books, Shaftesbury, 1994

Goelitz, Jeffrey, *The Ultimate Kid*, Planetary Publications, Boulder Creek, CA, 1986

Judson, Stephanie (ed), *A Manual on Nonviolence and Children*, New Society Publishers, BC, Canada, 1984 (Includes *For the Fun of it!* by Marta Harrison)

Lamont, Georgeanne and Sally Burns, *Values and Visions*, Manchester Development Education Project, Manchester, 1993

Liedloff, Jean, *The Continuum Concept: In Search of Happiness Lost*, Addison-Wesley Publishing Company, Reading, MA, 1985

Richardson, Robin and Angela Wood, *Inside Stories*, Trentham Books, Hanley, Stoke on Trent, 1992

Sandoz, Bobbie, *Parachutes For Parents: Learning to Parent From The Wisdom of Love*, Family Works Publications, Honolulu, Hawaii, 1993

Sokolov, Ivan and Deborah Hutton, *The Parents Book*, Thorsons Publishing, Wellingborough, Northants, 1988

Wichman, Frederick B, *Kauai Tales*, Bamboo Ridge Press, Honolulu, Hawaii, 1989

Useful Addresses

Most of these organizations are non-profit-making and would appreciate a stamped self-addressed envelope, return postage, or an international reply coupon – whichever is appropriate.

Sources for Stories and Tools

Animal Town Game Co
PO Box 485
Healdsburg
CA 95448
USA
   Cooperative board games and books.

Children's Book Press
1461 9th Ave
San Francisco
CA 94122
USA
   Multi-cultural literature.

Chinaberry Book Service
2780 Via Orange Way
Suite B
Spring Valley
CA 91978
USA
   Catalogue of books.

Creative Parenting
Parenting Press Inc
PO Box 75267
Seattle
WA 98125
USA
   Catalogue for parents.

Development Education Project
c/o Manchester Metropolitan University
801 Wilmslow Rd
Didsbury
Manchester M20 8RG
England, UK
   Values and Visions, guidelines for spiritual development
and global awareness in the classroom (but this can also be
used at home) for teachers and parents.

Family Pastimes
RR 4
Perth
Ontario
K7H 3C6
Canada
   Cooperative board games.

Hearthsong
PO Box B
Sebastopol
CA 95473
USA
  Catalogue for families.

Heartstone Story Circle
Longdon Court
Spring Gardens
Buxton
Derbyshire SK17 6BZ
Engalnd, UK
  Story circles of children and adults addressing the problems
of bullying and racism through the use of story. Around 2000
story circles nationwide. Pack provided for new groups.

The National Council for Self-Esteem
PO Box 277877
Sacramento
CA 95827
USA
  Membership organization with newsletter and
bibliography of self-esteem materials.

Planetary Publications
PO Box 66
Boulder Creek
CA 95006
USA
  Catalogue of books and tapes in the HeartMath system;
for children, teenagers and adults
  (Institute of HeartMath, PO Box 1463, Boulder Creek,
CA 95006, USA).

The Self-Esteem Store
3201 SW 15th St
Deerfield Beach
FL 33442
USA
Books and materials on self-esteem by mail order.

Teaching Tolerance
400 Washington Ave
Montgomery
AL 36104
USA
A free, twice-yearly magazine for teachers with resources/ideas for interracial harmony.

White Eagle Publishing Trust
New Lands
Liss
Hampshire GU33 7HY
England, UK
Publishers of spiritual teachings for children.

The Working Group Against Racism in Children's Resources
460 Wandsworth Road
London SW8 3LX
England UK
Guidelines and newsletter for the selection and evaluation of child development books.

Global Organizations

Amnesty International
322 Eighth Ave
New York
NY 10001
USA
  Provides human rights resources (books, video tapes, etc) for all ages.

Center for Environmental Education
881 Alma Real Drive
Suite 300
Pacific Palisades
CA 90272
USA
  Environmental education resource centre with newsletter, library and information searches.

Global Co-operation House
World Spiritual University
65 Pound Lane
London NW10 2HH
England UK
  One of over 3,000 centres in 62 countries. Offers educational programmes for the development of human, moral and spritual values. Affiliated to the United Nations.

Save the Children
17 Grove Lane
London SE5 8RD
England, UK
  Promotes the rights of children. Runs over 100 groups in the UK.

UN Publications
2 United Nations Plaza
Room DC2-853
New York
NY 10017
USA
   Offers a variety of posters, books and 'lesson plans' on peace education.

UNICEF UK
55 Lincoln's Inn Fields
London WC2A 3NB
England, UK
   Offers information and educational material on development issues.

World Wide Fund for Nature
Panda House
Weyside Park
Godalming
Surrey GU7 1XR
England, UK
   Previously World Wildlife Fund. Information and membership for adults and children.

Alternatives in Education

Alliance for Parental Involvement in Education
PO Box 59
East Chatham
NY 12060
USA
   Information, support, resources and networking for parental involvement in all education.

Alternative Education Resource Group
39 William St
Hawthorne
Victoria 3122
Melbourne
Australia
Organization supplying resources for alternative education.

The Alternative Education Resource Organization
417 Roslyn Rd
Roslyn Heights
NY 11577
USA
Helps those who want to change education to a more empowering and holistic form. Newsletter, with networking news from different realms of alternative, holistic education.

Canadian Alliance of Homeschoolers
RR1
St George
Ontario
NOE 1NO
Canada
Organization to support those who wish to educate their children at home.

Education Now
113 Arundel Drive
Bramcote Hills
Nottingham NG9 3FQ
England, UK
Aims to stimulate and inform alternative educational

debate through conferences, courses, consultancy, research
and publishing. Membership organization with newsletter.

Education Otherwise
5 Elm Gardens
Welwyn Garden City
Herts AL8 6RX
  Organization supporting parents who wish to educate
their children at home.

Growing Without Schooling
2269 Massachusetts Ave
Cambridge
MA 02140
USA
  John Holt Associates' newsletter for those who wish to
educate their children at home.

Homeschoolers Australia Pty Ltd
PO Box 420
Kellyville 2153
NSW
Australia
  Information for those who wish to educate their
children at home.

Human Scale Education
96 Carlingcott
Nr Bath
BA2 8AW
England, UK
  Organization to promote a partnership between home
and school, with parental involvement in all education.

The New Zealand Home Schooling Association
5 Thanet Ave
Mt Albert
Aukland
New Zealand
   Support organization for those who wish to educate their children at home.

Parent Support and Resources

Exploring Parenthood
Latimer Education Centre
194 Freston Road
London W10 6TT
England, UK
   Forum for parents and professionals to discuss common hurdles of parenting. Professionals available to run parent workshops throughout the country.

Mothers at Home
8310 Old Courthouse Rd
Vienna
VA 22182
USA
   Newsletter supporting mothers who choose to stay at home.

National Children's Bureau
8 Wakely St
London WC2B 5AU
England, UK
   Provides booklists on child care and development, and refers people to specific organizations.

National Children's Bureau of Australia
PO Box 686
Mulgrave North
Victoria 3170
Australia
Information, referrals and resources.

National Council for One Parent Familes
225 Kentish Town Road
London EC1V 7QE
England, UK
Information and training services for and concerning single parents and their children.

Parent Network
44–46 Caversham Road
London NW5 2DS
England, UK
Provides local support and education groups for parents.

Parents' Resource Connection
5102 Deerwood Lane
NE Bemidji
MN 56601
USA
Listing of publications and support groups for parents.

Parents Without Partners
PO Box 809250
Chicago
IL 60680
USA
Organization running support groups and activities for single parents and their children.

Index

anger 14–15
body
    effects of imagination 4
    effects of language 11–12
    effects of stress 4, 17
    effects of the heart 65
de-stressing hints 19–20
Einstein, Albert 104–105
emotions
    seeing and feeling 29–30
    understanding 23–24
environment 93
extended family 85
fairness 79–80
family tantrums 17–18
family values 2, 76–77
heart 2
    connecting with 30–31
    effects on the body 65
    Heart Answers 43–44
    journals of 31, 32
    relaxing into 18–19
    sending love and peace
        74–75, 82, 102–103
imagery
    and language 11–13
    personal 14
    as a tool 5

images 2–3, 5
    of children 16
imagination 2, 5
    and goal attainment 48
    effects of 3–4
language 11–13
legends 7–8
neck pains 11–12
Ohana 85
'pause button' 15, 31
perception
    clouds of 46–47
    effects on stress 4–5, 36–37
    switching 16–17
story-telling 7–8
stress
    effects on the body 4, 17
    effects of perception 4–5,
        36–37
    managing 17–20
support, unspoken 15
verbal abuse 11
worry 45